HOW MACHINES WORK

FAST CARS

IAN GRAHAM

W
FRANKLIN WATTS
LONDON•SYDNEY

An Appleseed Editions book

First published in 2008 by Franklin Watts

Franklin Watts
338 Euston Road, London NW1 3BH

Franklin Watts Australia
Level 17/207 Kent St, Sydney, NSW 2000

© 2008 Appleseed Editions

Appleseed Editions Ltd
Well House, Friars Hill, Guestling, East Sussex TN35 4ET

Created by Q2AMedia
Series Editor: Honor Head
Book Editor: Harriet McGregor
Senior Art Director: Ashita Murgai
Designers: Harleen Mehta, Ravijot Singh
Picture Researcher: Amit Tigga

ISBN 978 0 7496 8074 9

Dewey classification: 629.228

All words in **bold** can be found in Glossary on pages 30–31.

Website information is correct at time of going to press. However, the publishers cannot
accept liability for any information or links found on third-party websites.

A CIP catalogue for this book is available from the British Library.

Picture credits
t=top b=bottom c=centre l=left r=right m=middle
Cover Images: Main Image: ©BMW AG. Smaller Image tl: Porsche

Bugatti: 4, BMW: 5t, Mazda: 5b, Ferrari: 6, Mark Scheuern/ Alamy: 6 inset, Porsche: 8, 9t, Daimlerchrysler: 10, 11t,
BMW: 11b, Bugatti: 12, Transtock Inc./ Alamy: 13t, BMW: 13b, Graham Harrison/ Alamy: 14, Goodyear: 15, Ford: 16t,
BMW: 16b, Porche: 18t, Chris Alan Wilton/ Gettyimages: 18b, Porche: 19, Johannes Flex/ Shutterstock: 20, Motoring Picture
Library/ Alamy: 21t, Michael Shake/ Bigstockphoto: 21b, Daimlerchrysler: 22, Ford: 23, 25tr, 25ml, Transtock Inc./ Alamy:
25br, Mazda Automobiles: 26, NMGB: 27, 27 inset, Car Culture/ Corbis: 28t, SAAB Automobiles: 28b, Mark Scheuern/
Alamy: 29t, Mazda Automobiles: 29b

Q2AMedia Art Bank: 7, 9b, 17, 24b

Printed in Hong Kong

Franklin Watts is a division of Hachette Children's Books

CONTENTS

FAST CARS

Fast cars are designed to be more fun to drive than ordinary cars. Their size, weight, power and shape are chosen to give them a great performance on the road.

HOW FAST IS A FAST CAR?

The fastest cars on the roads have a top speed of about 400 kph , but a very high top speed is not all-important in a road car. A car that goes fast in a straight line may not be very good at cornering. Fast road cars have to be all-rounders. As well as being fast, they have to **accelerate**, corner and stop quickly, too.

▼ The Bugatti Veyron is the world's fastest **production car** – and one of the most expensive!

BUGATTI VEYRON 16.4

Specification

Engine:	8.0 l W16 turbocharged
Power:	1,001 horsepower (746 kW)
Acceleration:	0–100 kph (0–62 mph) in 2.5 seconds
Top speed:	407 kph (253 mph)

INSIDE A FAST CAR

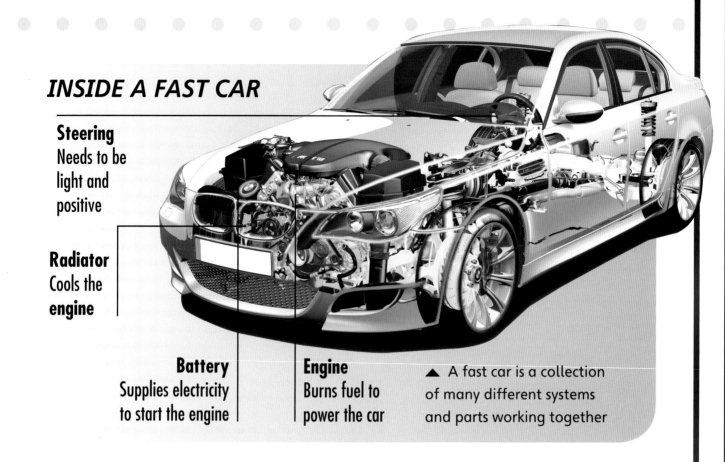

Steering
Needs to be light and positive

Radiator
Cools the engine

Battery
Supplies electricity to start the engine

Engine
Burns fuel to power the car

▲ A fast car is a collection of many different systems and parts working together

SPORTS AND SUPERS

There are two main types of fast road cars. Sports cars are small and light. Most sports cars have only two seats, because they are shorter than other cars. Being short and light allows them to make tight turns faster. Many sports cars are convertibles – their roof can be taken off or folded back.

Supercars are even faster. They have bigger, more powerful engines, and they look fantastic, too!

◀ The Mazda MX5 Miata is a classic two-seater sports car. It is small, light and close to the ground

A NOTE ABOUT SPEED
Fast cars are designed for speed, but also for safety. Even supercars MUST obey the speed limit!

ENGINE POWER

Fast cars depend on the design of their engines for their power and speed. The styling and weight of the cars also add to their fantastic performance.

▼ The powerful 8-cylinder engine and smooth lines of this Ferrari F430 make it one of today's top-performing supercars

FERRARI F430

Specification
Engine:	4.3 l V8
Power:	490 horsepower (365 kW)
Acceleration:	0–100 kph (0–62 mph) in 4.0 seconds
Top speed:	315 kph (196 mph)

HOW AN ENGINE WORKS

A car's engine produces the power to turn the wheels. Some fast cars have very big engines, but a big engine is not always needed. A small engine may be powerful enough for a small, light car. Inside the engine, explosions are caused by burning **fuel** in bottle-shaped **cylinders**. The explosions make **pistons** move up and down inside the cylinders. The up–down movements of the pistons make the car's wheels turn.

THE FOUR-STROKE CYCLE

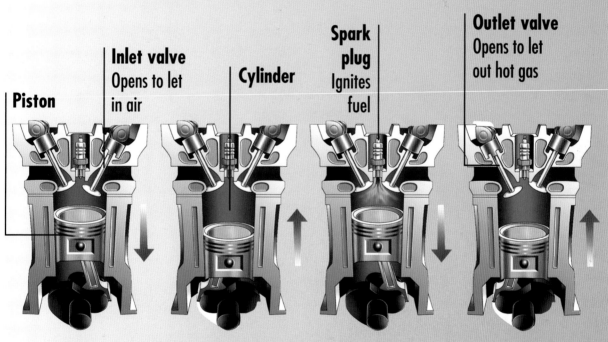

Piston

Inlet valve Opens to let in air

Cylinder

Spark plug Ignites fuel

Outlet valve Opens to let out hot gas

① *SUCK*

The piston moves down. The inlet valve opens. Air and fuel are sucked into the cylinder.

② *SQUEEZE*

The inlet valve closes. The piston moves up. Fuel and air are squeezed.

③ *BANG*

A spark from the spark plug ignites the fuel. The piston is forced back down the cylinder.

④ *BLOW*

The outlet valve opens. The piston rises. Hot gas is pushed out of the cylinder.

WHERE'S THE ENGINE?

When a car is designed, the engine is chosen to match its size, weight and speed. Most cars have their engine at the front, but the fastest cars often have their engine in the middle, behind the driver. The engine is the heaviest part of a car. Putting it in the middle shares out its weight more evenly between the wheels.

A car engine is a complicated machine with hundreds of moving parts. Slippery oil keeps them moving easily

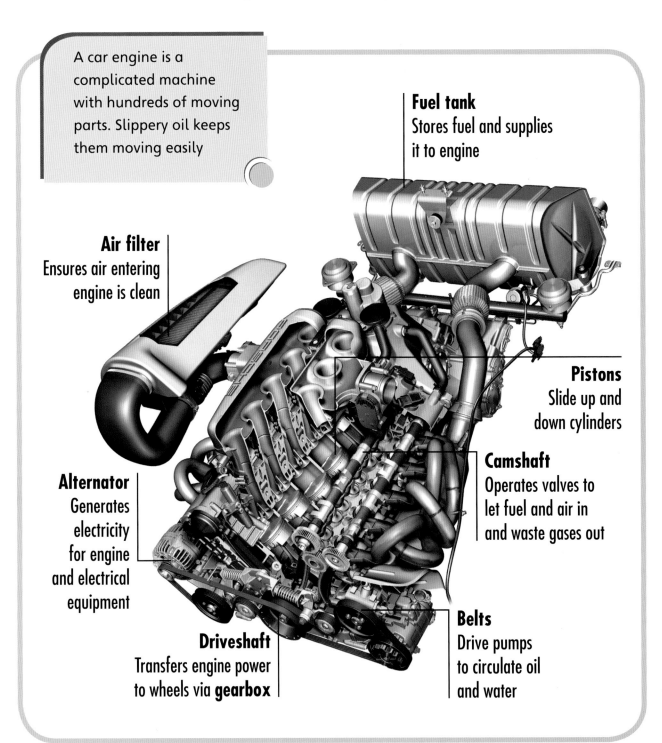

Fuel tank
Stores fuel and supplies it to engine

Air filter
Ensures air entering engine is clean

Pistons
Slide up and down cylinders

Camshaft
Operates valves to let fuel and air in and waste gases out

Alternator
Generates electricity for engine and electrical equipment

Driveshaft
Transfers engine power to wheels via **gearbox**

Belts
Drive pumps to circulate oil and water

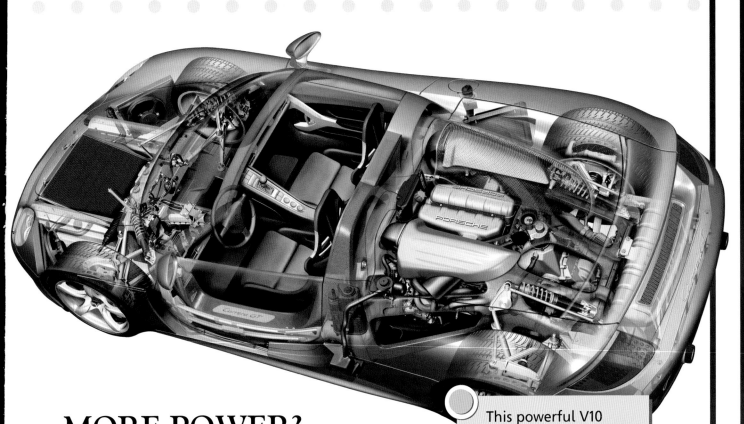

MORE POWER?

Most car engines burn petrol, but the fastest racing cars use a rocket fuel called nitromethane. If a car needs more power, it can be given an engine with more, or bigger, cylinders. Adding a part called a turbocharger produces even more power. It pushes extra air into the engine so it can burn fuel even faster.

This powerful V10 engine can take the Porsche Carrera GT from 0 to 200 kph in under 10 seconds

▶ Inside the turbocharger, exhaust gases from the car's engine drive a turbine which is linked to a compressor unit. The compressor sucks in extra air and forces it into the engine cylinders

(1) Exhaust gases from engine drive turbine

(2) Turbine drives compressor

(3) Compressor sucks in fresh air and forces it into engine

Turbine and compressor mounted on shared **axle**

THE POWERTRAIN

The huge power of a fast car's engine is sent to its wheels by a series of parts called the **powertrain**. This includes the **clutch**, the gearbox and the **differential**.

▼ A car's powertrain carries the engine power to the wheels

MERCEDES SLK 55 AMG

Specification

Engine:	5.4 l V8
Power:	360 horsepower (268 kW)
Acceleration:	0–100 kph (0–62 mph) in 4.9 seconds
Top speed:	250 kph (155 mph)

HOW THE POWERTRAIN WORKS

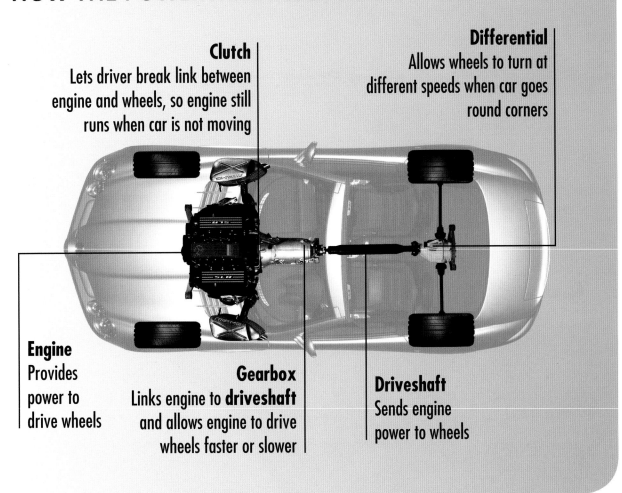

Clutch
Lets driver break link between engine and wheels, so engine still runs when car is not moving

Differential
Allows wheels to turn at different speeds when car goes round corners

Engine
Provides power to drive wheels

Gearbox
Links engine to **driveshaft** and allows engine to drive wheels faster or slower

Driveshaft
Sends engine power to wheels

GOING FASTER

A driver makes a car go faster by pressing the **accelerator**. This sends more fuel to the engine. To go even faster, the driver has to change **gear**. The gears are toothed wheels which interlock. When one gear turns, it turns the next gear. By choosing different gears to link the engine to the wheels, the driver can make the car go faster or slower.

▲ To go at different speeds, the driver changes gear by moving a gear stick. A car can have up to six gears including a reverse gear for going backwards

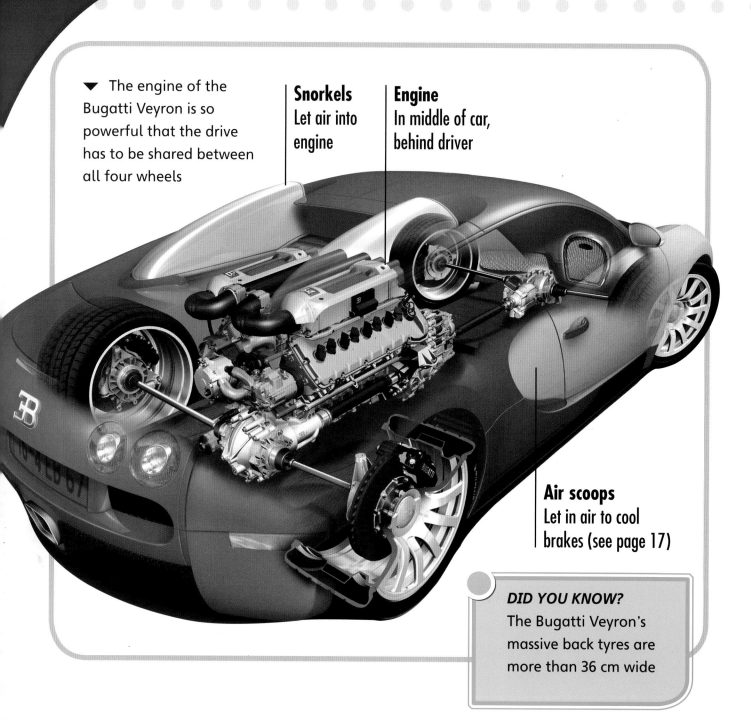

▼ The engine of the Bugatti Veyron is so powerful that the drive has to be shared between all four wheels

Snorkels
Let air into engine

Engine
In middle of car, behind driver

Air scoops
Let in air to cool brakes (see page 17)

DID YOU KNOW?
The Bugatti Veyron's massive back tyres are more than 36 cm wide

DRIVING THE WHEELS

Most fast car engines drive only two of the car's four wheels. A few supercars have engines so powerful that two wheels are not able to handle all the power. These cars have all-wheel drive. All four wheels are driven by the engine. Only the most powerful supercars use all-wheel drive because the parts add extra weight to the car.

LAMBORGHINI MURCIELAGO LP640

Specification

Engine:	6.5 I V12
Power:	640 horsepower (471kW)
Acceleration:	0–100 kph (0–62 mph) in 3.4 seconds
Top speed:	340 kph (210 mph)

▼ The all-wheel-drive Lamborghini Murcielago

AUTOMATIC AND MANUAL

In a car with an **automatic gearbox**, the gear changes automatically as the driver accelerates or decelerates. In other cars, the driver changes gear by moving a gear stick. Instead of a gear stick, some fast cars have switches called **paddles** on the steering wheel. Pressing one paddle changes up a gear. Pressing the other paddle changes down a gear.

Paddle switches

▶ The steering wheel of the BMW M5 has paddle switches for changing gear

WHEELS AND TYRES

A car's tyres have two important jobs. They support the weight of the car and they use the power of the engine to move the car.

HOW TYRES WORK

A car's tyres are made of air-filled rubber. Tyres are made of rubber because this soft material grips the road well. If water gets between the tyres and the road, it stops the tyres from gripping. The car will **skid** and the driver will not be able to steer or **brake**. The zigzag grooves in a car's tyres are called the **tread**. On a wet surface, the tread allows water to be squeezed out from under the tyre.

▼ Car tyres have to grip the road, even when the surface is covered with water

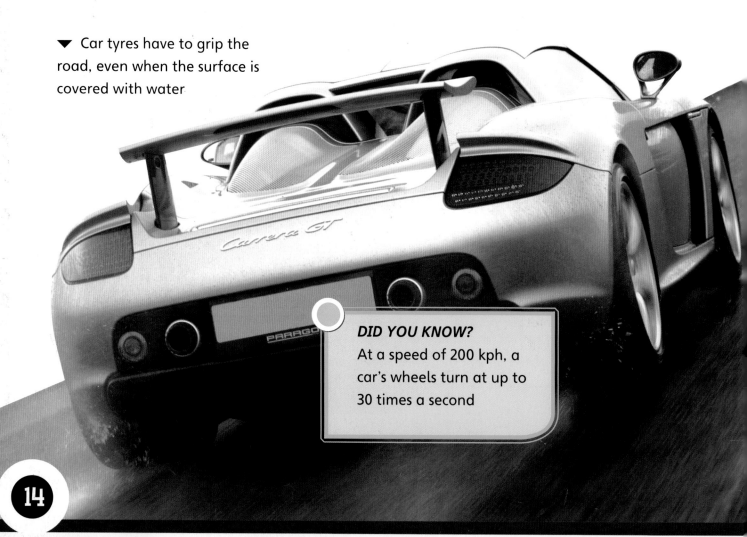

DID YOU KNOW?
At a speed of 200 kph, a car's wheels turn at up to 30 times a second

INSIDE A TYRE

Cap plies
Hold other layers in place

Body plies
Made of fabric covered with rubber

Tread
Made from natural and man-made rubber

Sidewall
Protects body plies and stops air from escaping

Metal rim
Bolted to axle of car

Steel belts
Strengthen area beneath tread

▲ Fabric, steel and rubber give a tyre the right amount of strength and flexibility

▶ A car tyre fits tightly into grooves around the metal rim of the wheel

SUSPENSION

A car's wheels are linked to the rest of the car by sets of springs. These springy links are called the **suspension** system. They let the wheels move up and down over bumps in the ground, while the rest of the car moves along more smoothly. The air-filled tyres help to cushion the car from small bumps, too.

Coil spring
Squashes up and springs back as wheels go over bumps

Steering link
Connects wheel to steering system

▼ The coiled springs of a car's suspension system give a smooth ride for the driver and passengers

DID YOU KNOW?
An average driver uses a car's brakes about 75,000 times a year

HOW DO CARS STOP?

A driver slows a car by pressing the brake pedal. This makes a pair of tough pads squeeze together and grip a disc, which is attached to the wheel and which turns with it. Gripping the disc slows the wheel down and so slows down the whole car. This type of brake is called a **disc brake**.

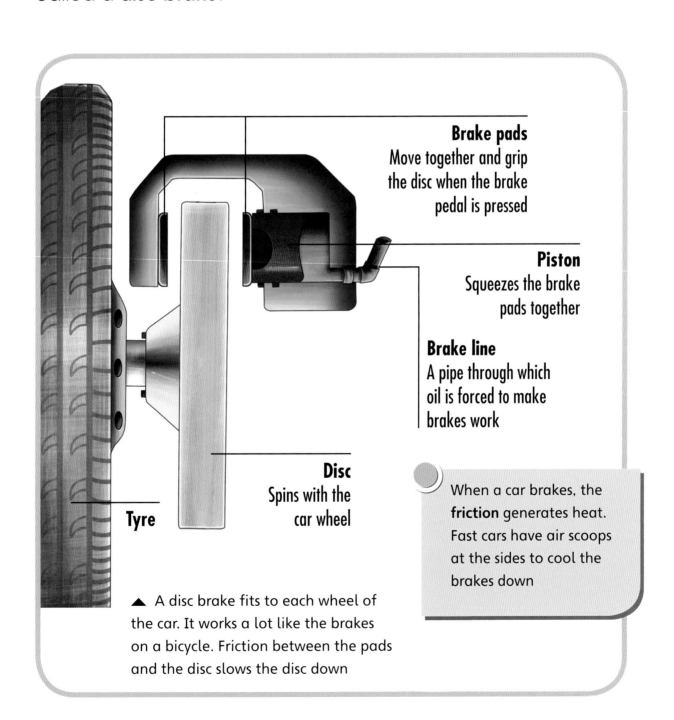

Brake pads
Move together and grip the disc when the brake pedal is pressed

Piston
Squeezes the brake pads together

Brake line
A pipe through which oil is forced to make brakes work

Disc
Spins with the car wheel

Tyre

When a car brakes, the **friction** generates heat. Fast cars have air scoops at the sides to cool the brakes down

▲ A disc brake fits to each wheel of the car. It works a lot like the brakes on a bicycle. Friction between the pads and the disc slows the disc down

SHAPE AND BUILD

A fast car has a low, smooth, gently curving shape so that air can flow around it easily. This helps it to go as fast as possible and to use less fuel.

SHAPED FOR SPEED

When a fast car moves through the air, the air pushes back. If a car is the wrong shape, the air pushes back and slows it down. This is called **air resistance**, or **drag**. If a car is the right shape, air flows around it easily and the car can go much faster.

▶ This Porsche Cayman S has a **streamlined** shape which lowers air resistance

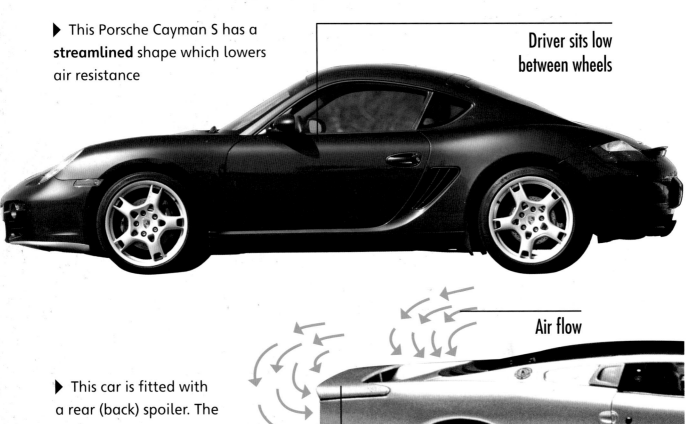

Driver sits low between wheels

Air flow

▶ This car is fitted with a rear (back) spoiler. The spoiler creates a high-pressure area that pushes down on the rear of the car and helps it to go faster

Spoiler

THE WIND TUNNEL TEST

The shape of a fast car is tested in a **wind tunnel**. A car, or a model of it, is placed inside the tunnel. Air is then blown through the tunnel. The way the air flows around the car is measured. One way to see how air flows around a car in a wind tunnel is to use smoke. The flowing air is invisible, but streams of smoke blowing with the air can be seen by the human eye.

▼ Smoke shows how air flows around a car in a wind tunnel test

DID YOU KNOW?
Wind tunnels have been used to test the shape of vehicles since the 1890s

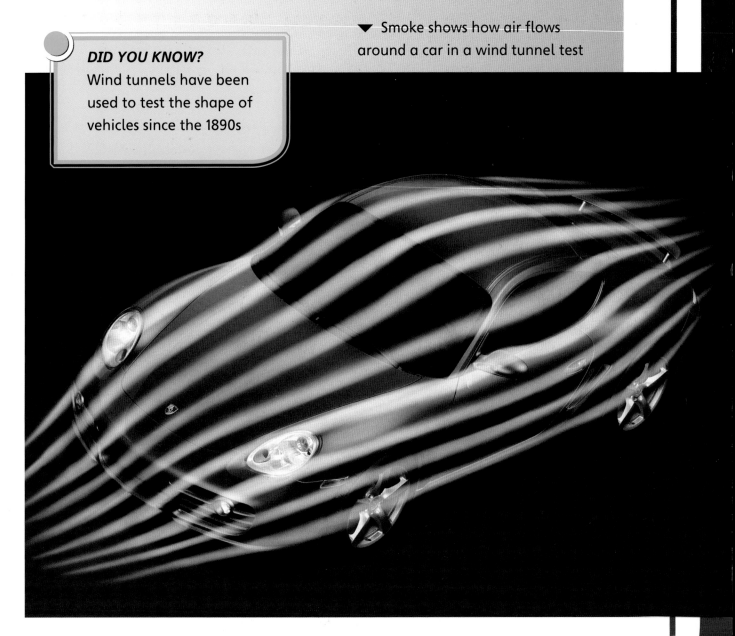

WHAT ARE CARS MADE OF?

Most cars are made of steel, a strong metal that can be bent into any shape. Because steel is heavy, some parts of a car are made from lighter metals, such as aluminium, to reduce the weight. Aluminium is only one-third as strong as steel, but it is much lighter and does not rust.

BMW Z4 COUPE 3.0si SPORT

Specification

Engine:	3.0 l inline 6
Power:	265 horsepower (197 kW)
Acceleration:	0–100 kph (0–62 mph) in 5.7 seconds
Top speed:	250 kph (155 mph)

Windscreen
Made of safety glass

Bonnet
Made of aluminium to save weight

▲ The BMW Z4 sports car is a superb example of precision engineering

Body
Made of steel for strength

Tough metallic paint finish
Protects steel body against rust

CARBON CARS

The fastest cars are often made from materials that are lighter than steel. Some sports cars have a body made of plastic. Supercars are often made from a material called **carbon fibre**. To make a carbon-fibre part for a car, mats of woven carbon fibres are laid in a mould and soaked in liquid plastic, which sets hard. This material is very strong and light.

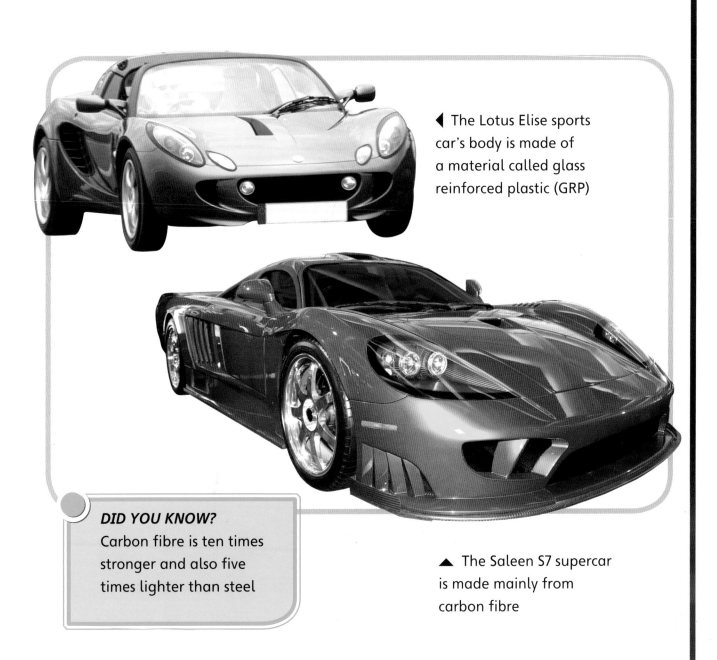

◀ The Lotus Elise sports car's body is made of a material called glass reinforced plastic (GRP)

DID YOU KNOW?
Carbon fibre is ten times stronger and also five times lighter than steel

▲ The Saleen S7 supercar is made mainly from carbon fibre

SAFETY FIRST

As well as being exciting to drive, fast cars are designed to be safe at high speeds. They have built-in safety features to protect the driver and passengers.

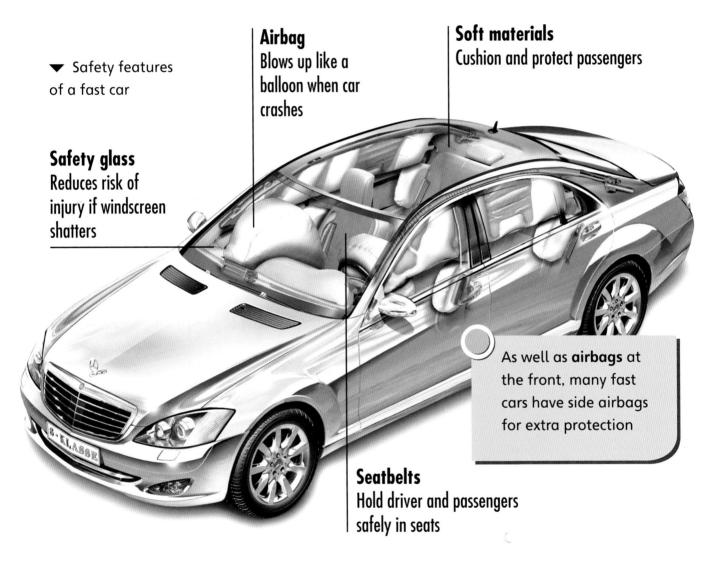

▼ Safety features of a fast car

Airbag
Blows up like a balloon when car crashes

Soft materials
Cushion and protect passengers

Safety glass
Reduces risk of injury if windscreen shatters

As well as **airbags** at the front, many fast cars have side airbags for extra protection

Seatbelts
Hold driver and passengers safely in seats

SAFE DESIGN

If a fast-moving car is involved in a crash, seatbelts protect the driver and passengers by holding them safely in their seats. They also spread the impact of a crash over a person's whole body, so there is less risk of injury.

▼ The part of a fast car where the driver and passengers sit is made extra-strong for safety

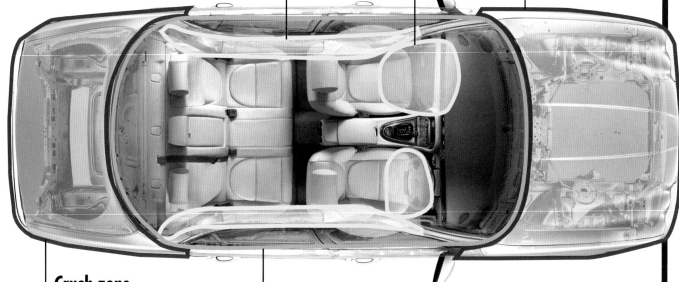

Side and front airbags
Blow up instantly if car is in a crash

Crush zone

Crush zone
Crumples first in collision to absorb impact

Safety cell
Strengthened to protect driver and passengers

SUPERCAR SAFETY

The fastest road cars have some of the same safety features as racing cars. In case of a serious crash, a racing car driver sits inside a super-strong tub, called a **safety cell**. The fastest road cars have a safety cell, too. Other parts of the car at the front and back are made weaker than the safety cell. In a crash, these weaker parts are designed to crumple first to protect the driver and passengers.

HOW AN AIRBAG WORKS

When a car hits something, airbags instantly blow up like balloons inside the car to protect the driver and passengers. The car measures how fast the car stops and can tell the difference between braking hard and a crash. If it decides the car is in a crash, it sets off a device that releases a lot of gas very quickly. This blows up the airbag, which acts like a cushion.

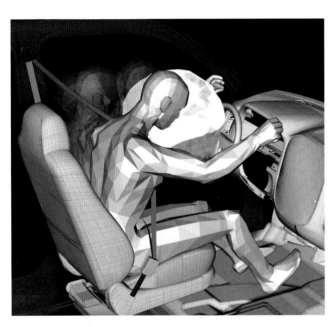

◀ In a collision, the airbag instantly inflates, protecting the driver's head from injury

DID YOU KNOW?
A car airbag blows up in 0.8 seconds – faster than the blink of an eye!

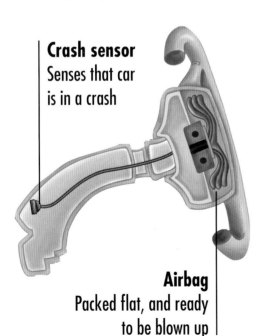

Crash sensor
Senses that car is in a crash

Airbag
Packed flat, and ready to be blown up

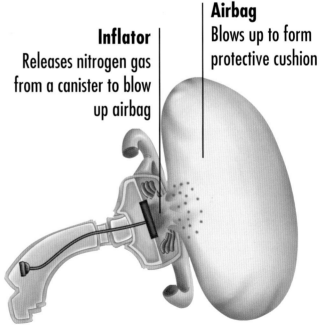

Inflator
Releases nitrogen gas from a canister to blow up airbag

Airbag
Blows up to form protective cushion

TESTING FOR SAFETY

In safety tests, **crash test dummies** sit in the cars. The dummies are built like people. Their movements and the forces acting on them are measured to find out what would happen to people in a real crash.

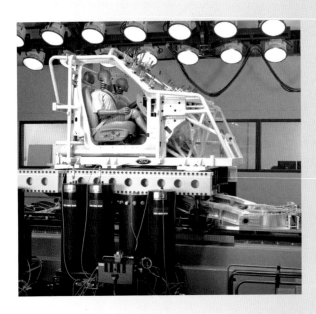

▲ 'Dummies are used in a specially designed **crash simulator** to see what would happen in a real car crash

◀ The effects of a real car crash are tested on dummies in a specially designed **crash simulator**

SPOT THE CAMERA!

If the engine is at the back of a car, it can be hard for the driver to see behind for reversing. As well as the normal mirrors, the Saleen S7 supercar has a camera at the back, which sends a picture to a screen in the car. Can you spot the camera?

Answer: just above the space between the 'L' and the 'E' of 'SALEEN'.

FUTURE CARS

The cars of the future are already being designed today! New ideas that may be used in the future are tested by building vehicles called **concept cars**.

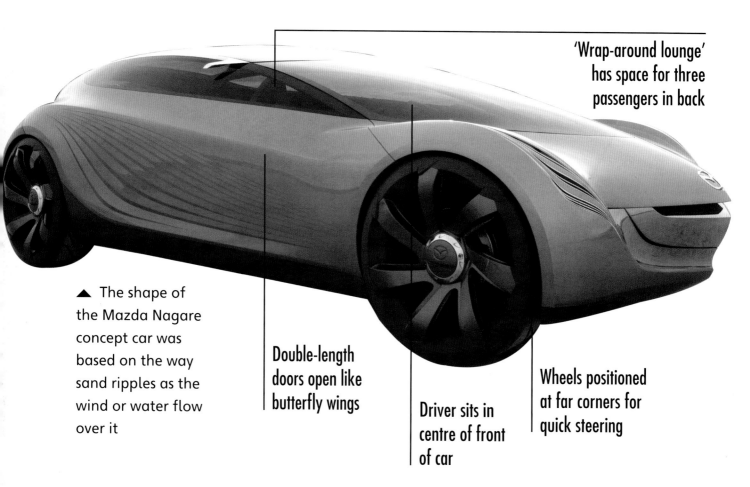

'Wrap-around lounge' has space for three passengers in back

▲ The shape of the Mazda Nagare concept car was based on the way sand ripples as the wind or water flow over it

Double-length doors open like butterfly wings

Driver sits in centre of front of car

Wheels positioned at far corners for quick steering

THINKING AHEAD

Concept cars are not built in large numbers and cannot be bought by the public. They are experimental cars. Many of them cannot even be driven, because they have no engine. They are put on display at motor shows around the world to see what people think of them. If the ideas tested in a concept car turn out to be popular, they may be built into future cars.

INSIDE A CONCEPT CAR

Designers of concept cars often like to play with new ideas. Why not have the controls operated by the driver's voice instead of switches? Why not have instruments which talk to the driver instead of the driver having to look at them? Why not put the driver's seat in the middle of the car instead of one side?

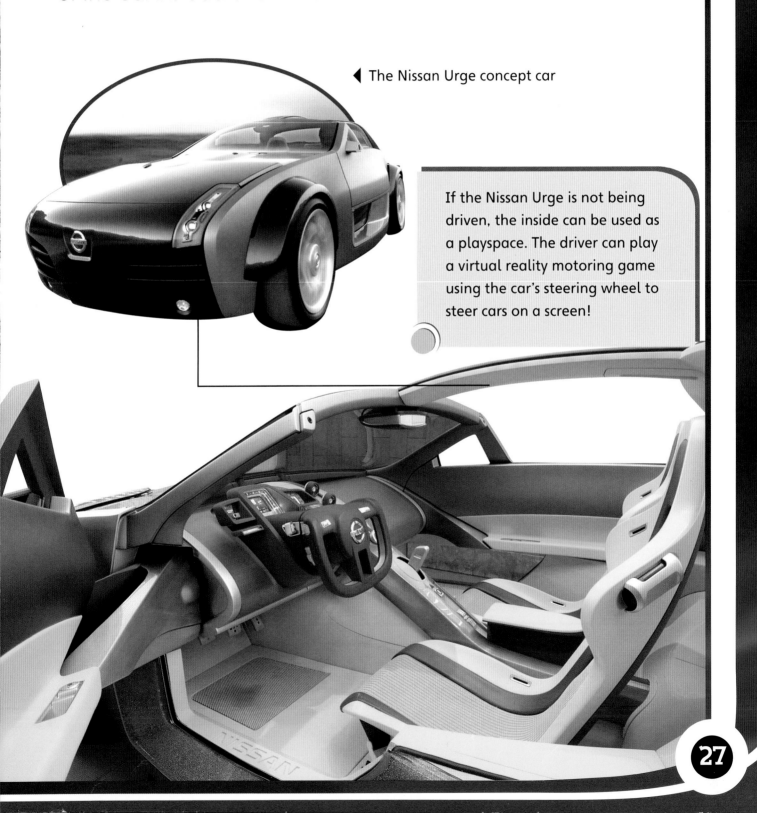

◀ The Nissan Urge concept car

If the Nissan Urge is not being driven, the inside can be used as a playspace. The driver can play a virtual reality motoring game using the car's steering wheel to steer cars on a screen!

IS IT A CAR? IS IT A PLANE?

Designers of concept cars sometimes use materials and shapes borrowed from other types of vehicles – especially aircraft. Planes and cars are alike in some ways. Although planes fly and cars go along the ground, they both travel through the air and they both have to be steered. The insides of some concept cars look very like aircraft cockpits.

Curved windscreen gives driver full 180-degree vision

▼ The roof, windscreen and sides of the Saab Aero-X are made in one piece, like a jet-fighter's cockpit cover

▼ The dashboard of the Saab Aero-X displays information on glowing screens

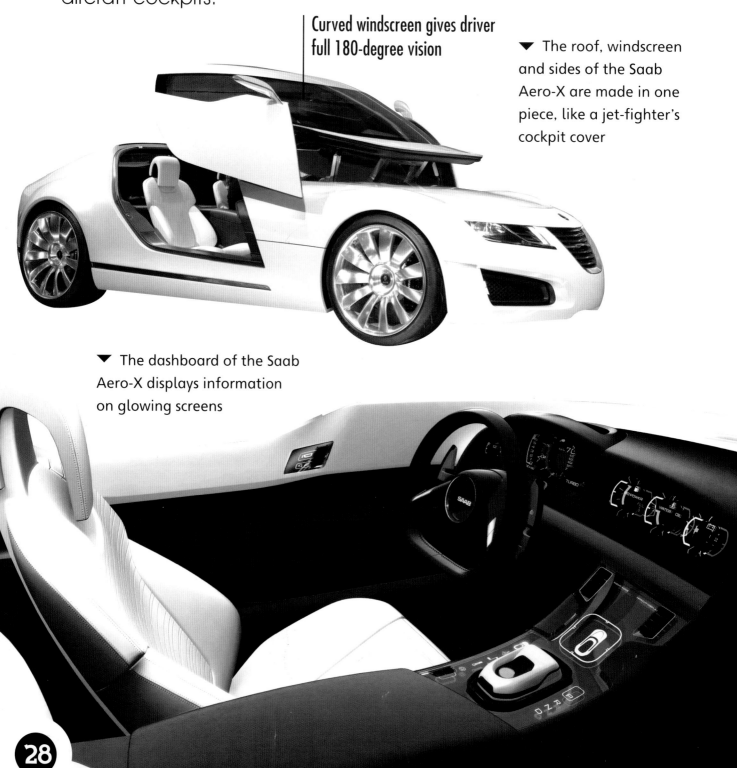

GULL-WING AND SCISSOR DOORS

Instead of opening in the usual way, some concept cars have doors that slide open sideways or lift upwards. Car doors that swing upwards are known as gull-wing doors because they look like a bird's wings. Sometimes there are no doors at all, because the whole top of the car opens up.

▶ This Ford Mustang concept car has doors called scissor doors because of the way they open

DID YOU KNOW?
The Alfa Romeo Spix is a concept car that is designed to fly!

◀ The gull-wing doors of the Mazda Ryuga allow both sides of the car to swing open

GLOSSARY

Accelerate
To go faster

Accelerator A pedal which is pressed to make the car go faster

Airbag A safety device that blows up to protect the driver or passenger

Air resistance
When air pushes back against a moving car

Alternator
A part of a car that supplies electricity for the engine and equipment

Automatic gearbox
A type of gearbox that changes gear on its own

Axle The metal rod on which wheels are fixed

Battery The part that supplies electricity to a motor

Brake To slow down a car; the part that slows or stops the car

Carbon fibre
A strong, light material used to make some fast cars

Concept car
An experimental car built to show or test new ideas

Clutch The part that allows the driver to break the link between the engine and wheels

Crash test dummy
A model used to test how safe a car is

Crash simulator
Machine for testing what happens in a real car crash

Cylinder The part of a car engine where fuel is burned

Differential A set of gears that lets the wheels turn at different speeds when a car goes round a corner

Disc brake A type of brake where pads are squeezed together to slow the wheel down

Drag See Air resistance

Driveshaft A metal bar that carries a car's engine power to its wheels

Engine The machine that burns fuel to provide the power needed to make a car move

Friction The effect produced when one surface rubs against another

Fuel Liquid burned in a car's engine to provide power

Gear A toothed wheel

Gearbox A set of gears that allow the engine to drive the wheels at different speeds

Paddles Gear switches on steering wheel

Piston The part of a car engine that is forced up and down inside a cylinder

Powertrain The parts of a car that link the engine to the wheels

Radiator The part that helps to cool the car's engine by letting heat escape

Safety cell The strong part of a car, built to protect people in a crash

Skid To slide out of control

Snorkel A tube through which air passes

Streamlined Shaped so that air flows around easily

Supercar A very fast, high-performance road car

Suspension The springy links between the wheels and the rest of the car

Tread The grooves in a car's tyres

Tyre The air-filled rubber tube around a car's wheel

Wind tunnel Equipment for studying how a car's shape affects air resistance

INDEX

Websites

http://www.chevroncars.com/learn/cars/car-fun-facts
Fun facts about cars

http://auto.howstuffworks.com/bugatti.htm
Learn more about the amazing Bugatti Veyron supercar.

http://www.sportscarcup.com/concept-cars
Great pictures of concept cars